The Nature Kid's Guide to
COWS

DAVID ANDERSON

LP Media Inc. Publishing
Text copyright © 2026 by LP Media Inc.
All rights reserved.

For information address LP Media Inc. Publishing,
30012 Variolite St NW, Princeton MN 55371
www.lpmedia.org

Publication Data

Cows
The Nature Kid's Guide to Cows — First edition.

Summary: "Learn all about Cows, the Nature Kid Way"
— Provided by publisher.

ISBN: 979-8-89818-186-4

[1. Cows – Non-Fiction] I. Title.

Title: The Nature Kid's Guide to Cows

CONTENTS

BARN BUDDIES

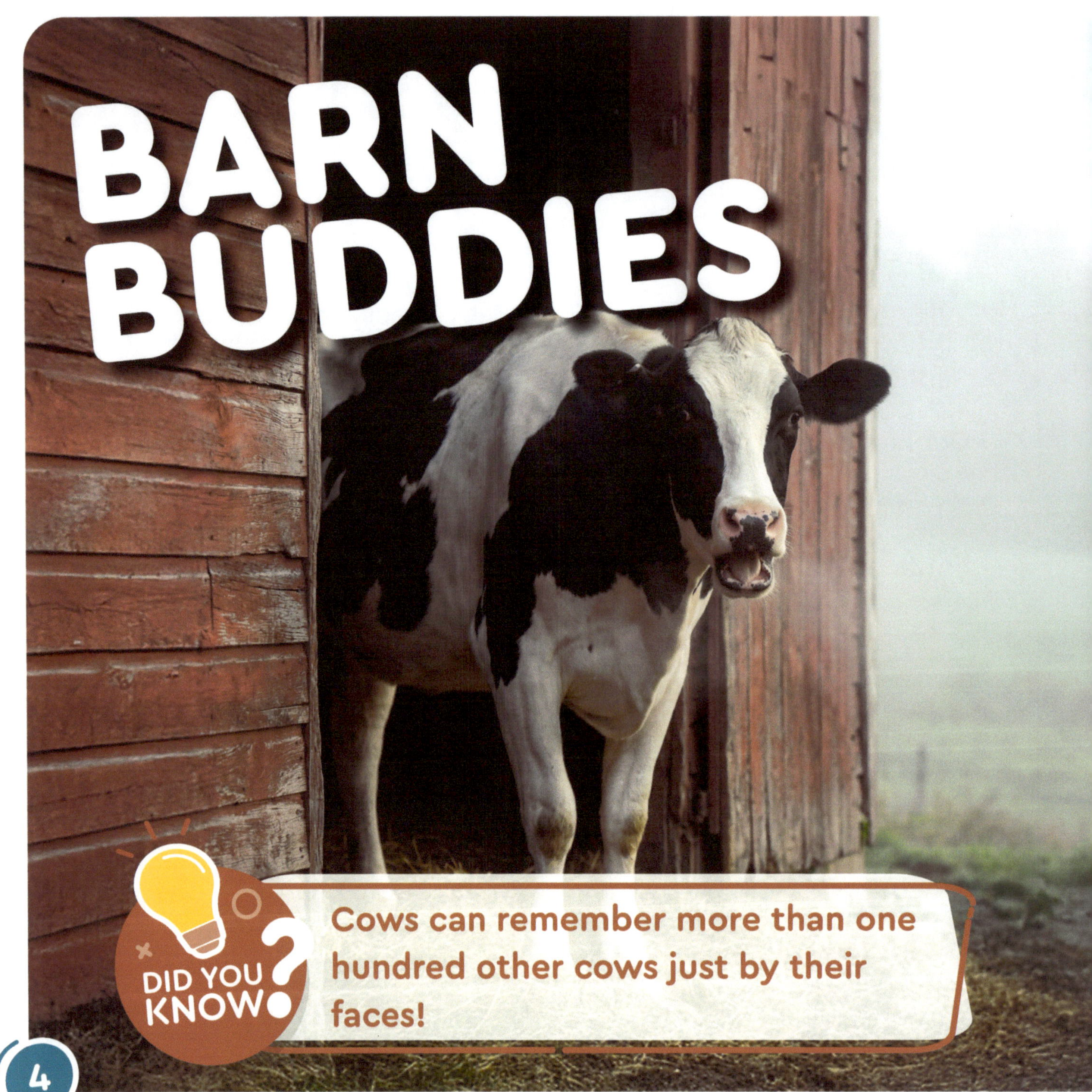

Cows can remember more than one hundred other cows just by their faces!

Moo! A black and white Holstein cow calls out from the big red barn.

Cows live on farms all over the world. They spend their days grazing in green fields. At night, many rest in a warm barn.

Farmers take good care of their cows. They give them fresh water and hay. They keep the barn clean and cozy.

Some cows are raised for their meat, others for milk. These are called dairy cows. The most popular dairy cow in the United States is the Holstein.

A farm can have just a few cows or many hundreds. Some cows have names, while others have numbers. Farmers get to know every one.

WILD ROOTS

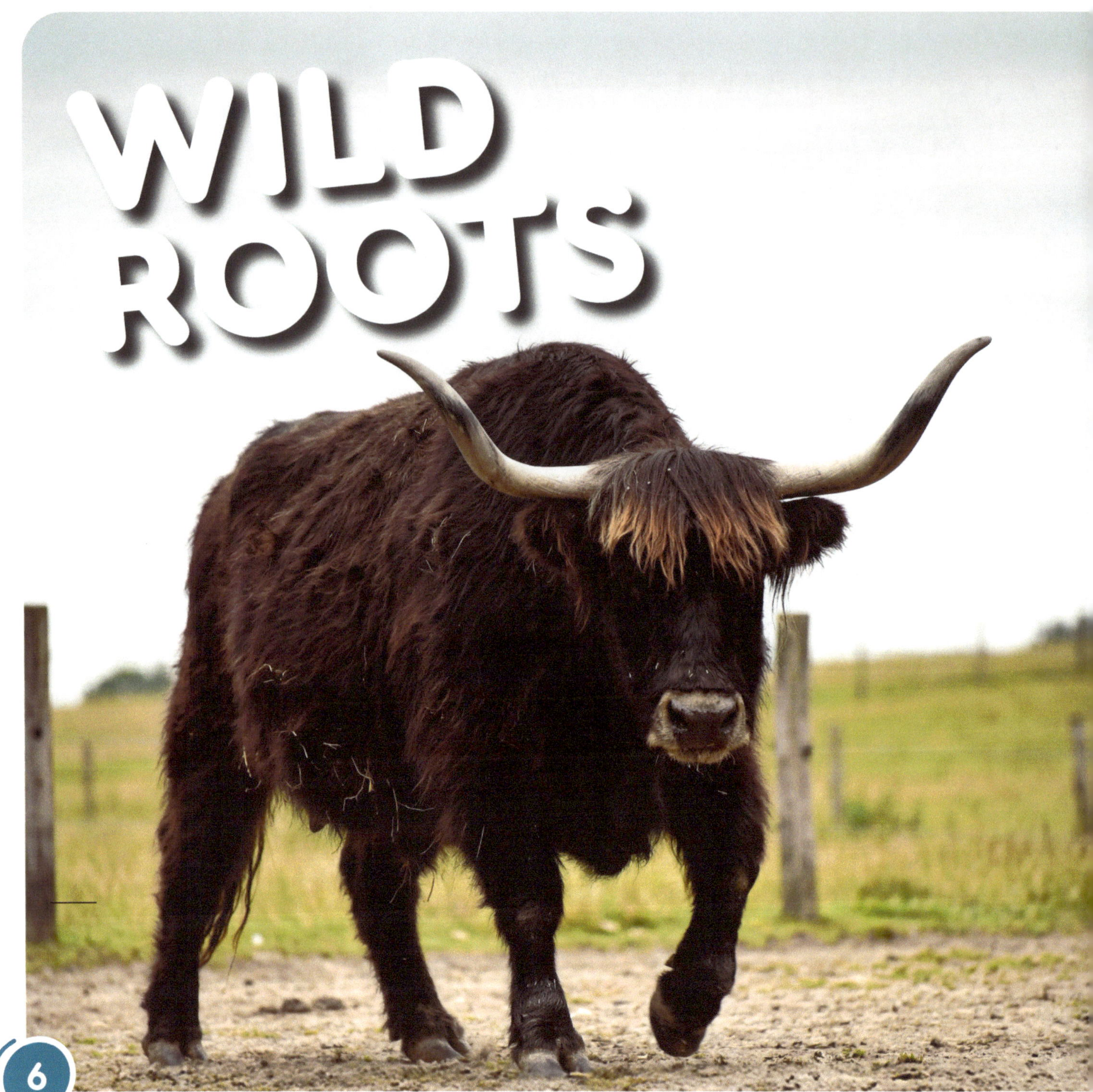

Thud! A big bull stamps its hooves on the ground.

Long ago, wild cattle roamed the earth's forests and grasslands.

They were much bigger than today's cows. They had long, curved horns. People began to tame them about ten thousand years ago.

Over time, those wild cattle became the farm cows we know. Highland cows still look a bit wild with their shaggy fur and long horns.

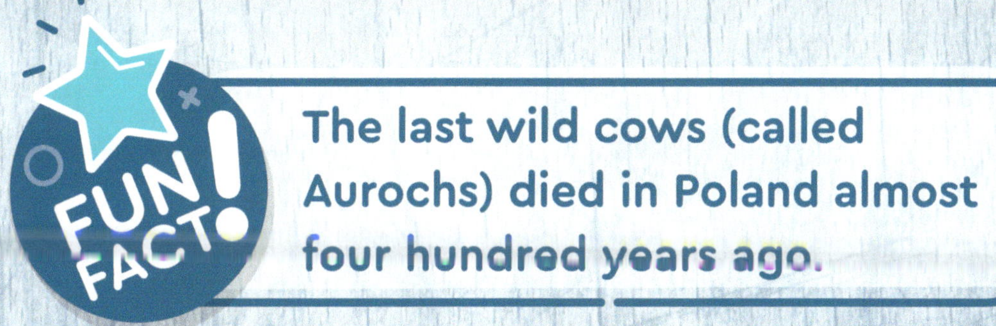

SUPER SIZED
FUN FACT!
The tallest cow ever was over six feet tall at the shoulder!
8

Whomp! A Belgian Blue cow plops down and the whole ground shakes.

A full-grown cow can weigh over 1,200 pounds. That's as big as a small car. Some cows can grow even heavier!

Belgian Blue cows are one of the biggest breeds. Their muscles are thick and round. They look super strong! They are called the body-builders of the cow world!

Most cows stand about five feet tall at the shoulder. That is taller than most second graders. Next to a cow, you would look very small.

COOL COW PARTS

Swish! A Texas Longhorn flicks its long tail to shoo away the flies.

Cows have some really cool body parts. Their tails work like fly swatters. One quick swish keeps pesky bugs away.

Texas Longhorn cows have the most amazing horns. Their horns can stretch wider than six feet across!

Cows have a special stomach with four parts. Food moves slowly from one part to the next. This helps cows break down the tough grass they eat.

A cow has no top front teeth — it has a tough, rubbery pad instead!

SNIFF AND SEE
12

Sniff! An Angus cow lifts its big wet nose to smell the air.

Cows have very sharp senses. Their big eyes sit on the sides of their head. This lets them see almost all the way around!

A cow's nose is always a bit wet. The wetness helps them pick up smells. Cows can smell things up to six miles away!

Cows hear well too. Their ears can turn to catch sounds from any direction. A small noise far off does not fool them.

SPOTS OR STRIPES

Splat! Mud lands on a Hereford cow's bright red and white coat.

There are over one thousand breeds of cows in the world. Some are big. Some are small. They come in many colors and patterns.

Hereford cows have red bodies and white faces. Holsteins have black and white patches. No two Holsteins have the same pattern, it's like their fingerprints!

Some cows have spots, and some are one solid color. Angus cows are all black or all red. Each breed has its own special look.

GRASS
GUZZLERS

Rip! A Highland cow tears up a big mouthful of fresh green grass.

Cows eat a lot of food each day. A single cow can munch through about forty pounds of grass and hay. That is like eating a bathtub full of salad!

Cows use their tongues to pull grass and their lower teeth to cut it. They wrap their tongue around it and pull. A cow's tongue is typically about twelve inches long.

To help digest all that grass, cows need to drink a lot of water. Up to 30 gallons a day during the summer!

A cow's tongue is so rough and strong it feels like sandpaper!

17

MOO MILK

Squirt! Holstein cows are lined up to be milked at the dairy.

Holstein cows are the top milk makers. One Holstein can give about eight gallons of milk a day. That is more than a hundred glasses!

Milk is used to make many yummy foods. Cheese, butter, yogurt, and ice cream all start as milk. Even some candy has milk in it.

Cows also give us leather for shoes and belts. Their soft hair can be used to make brushes. Cows give us more than most people think!

It takes about three gallons of milk to make just one gallon of ice cream!

MOO TALK

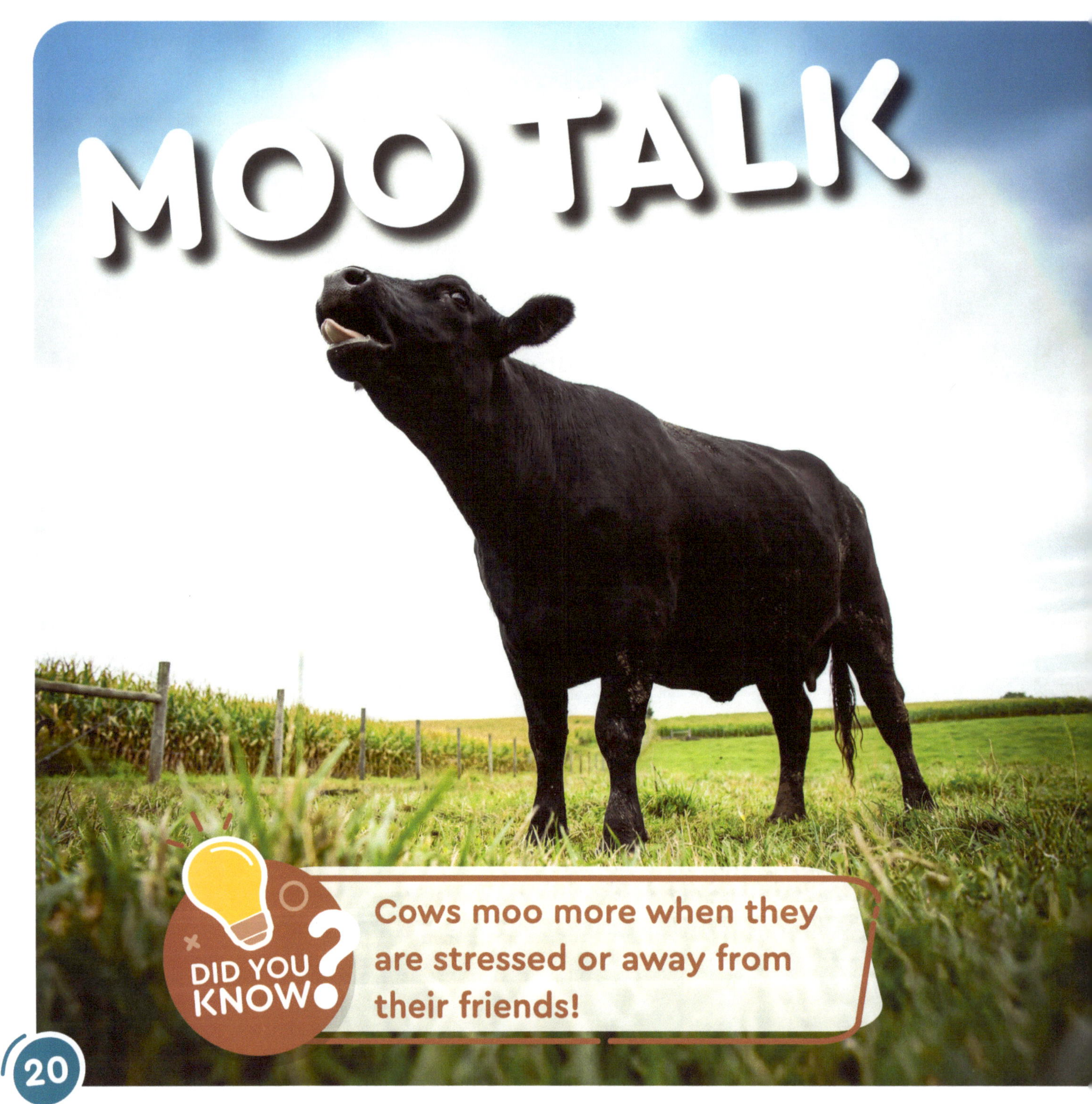

Cows moo more when they are stressed or away from their friends!

Moooo! A mother cow sends a loud call across the wide open field.

Cows talk to each other in many ways. They moo, grunt, and huff. Each sound means something different. Scientists have found that cows make different sounds depending on how they feel: happy, hungry, or stressed.

A loud, long moo often means a cow is looking for its calf. A short, soft moo might be a greeting. Cows can even tell each other's voices apart.

Cows also use their bodies to talk. They bump heads when they are upset. A calm cow will lick a friend to say hello.

DAY BY DAY

Clang! The pasture gate swings open and the cows walk back in.

Cows love having the same routine every day. They wake up early and head out to **graze**. After eating, they find a shady spot to rest.

Twice a day, dairy cows line up to be milked. They often walk to the barn in the same order each time. Each cow seems to know its place in line.

At night, cows settle down to rest again. They may sleep lying down or standing up. Most cows sleep only about four hours a day.

Dairy cows get grumpy when they are milked even a little bit late!

CLIP CLOP

DID YOU KNOW?
Cows can walk up stairs, but they have a hard time going down!

Clip clop! A Longhorn's heavy hooves beat the dusty dirt path.

Cows may look slow, but they can move fast when they want to. They walk, trot, and even gallop. Most cows can run faster than a person.

Each hoof has a hard shell, almost like a shoe. The bottom is tough and helps cows grip the ground. Hooves grow all the time, just like your nails.

Texas Longhorn cows once roamed huge open ranges. Cowboys drove giant herds across the plains, but a clap of thunder could set off a stampede – thousands of cows bolting at once, shaking the ground like an earthquake.

CHEW AND SNOOZE

DID YOU KNOW?

A cow moves its jaw about forty thousand times a day just chewing!

Chomp! A Highlander cow sits and chews the same bite again.

Cows are champion chewers. They chew their food and swallow it. Then they bring it back up. They chew it all over again! This is called chewing **cud**.

A cow chews cud for about eight hours a day. That is like chewing gum from breakfast until dinner. All that chewing helps break down tough plants.

When cows are not eating, they love to rest. They close their eyes and relax their jaws. A resting cow looks very peaceful and calm.

HERD LIFE

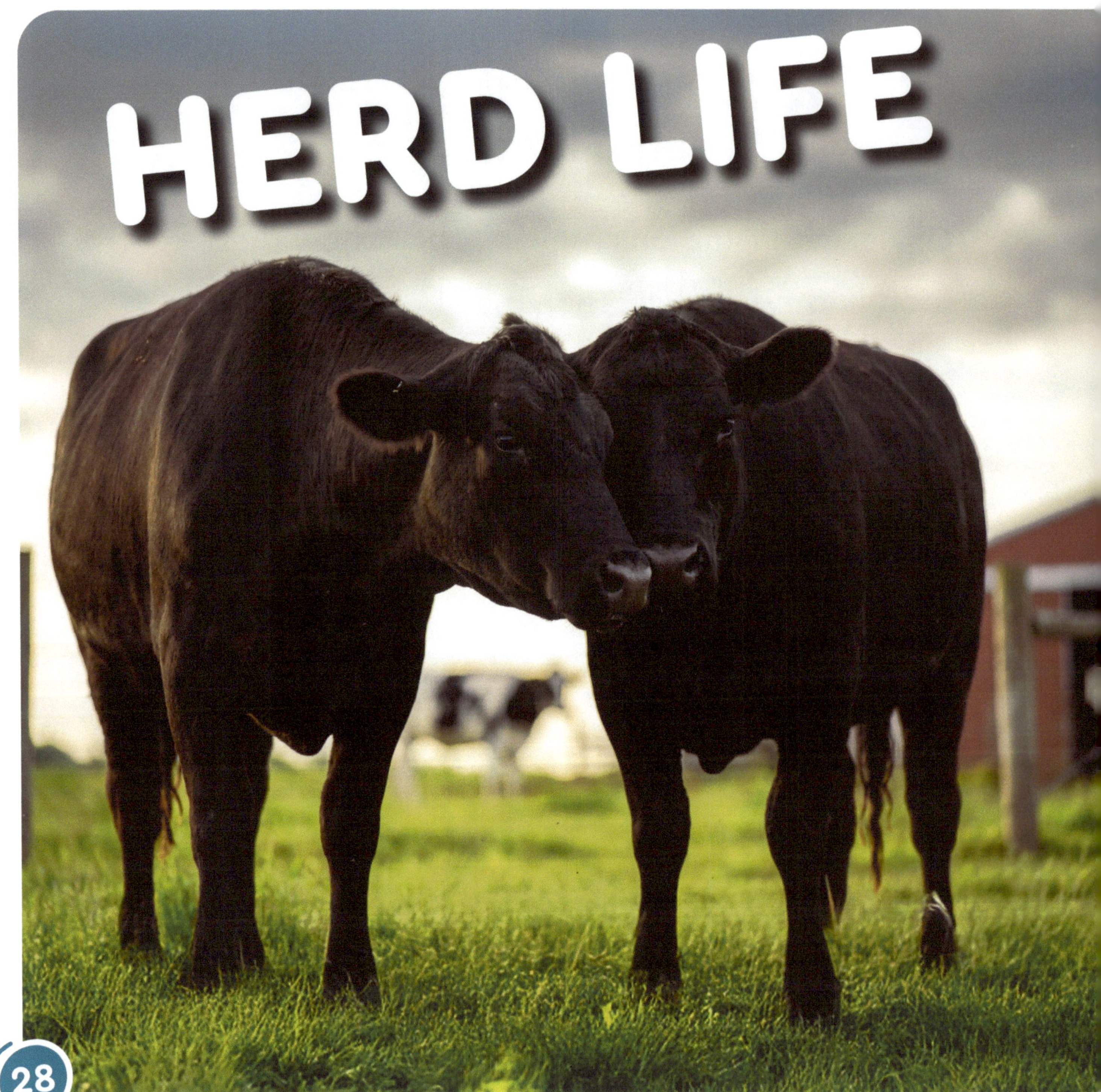

Bump! Two cows press their big heads together in the field.

Cows are very social animals. They like to be near other cows. A group of cows is called a **herd**.

Inside a herd, one cow is the boss. She gets to eat and drink first. The other cows step aside and follow her lead.

Cows make close friends within the herd. They groom each other and stand side by side. If a friend leaves the herd, a cow can feel sad.

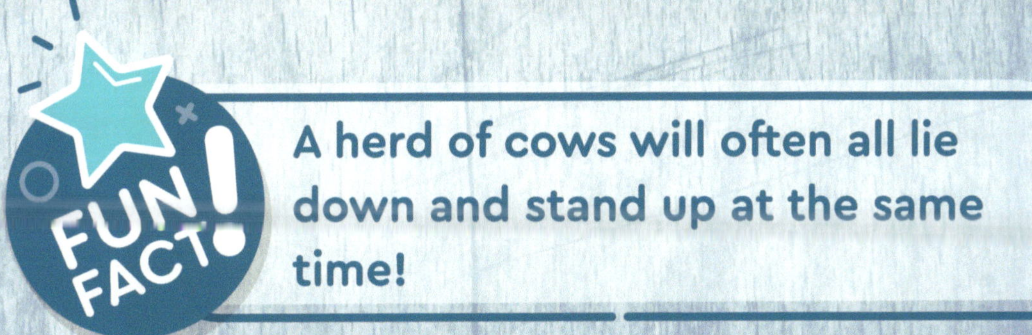

BABY TIME

FUN FACT!
A newborn calf weighs between 60–100 pounds at birth!

Thump, thump! A tiny calf kicks inside its mother's belly.

A mother cow carries her baby for about nine months. That is the same amount of time as a human mom. The baby grows safe and warm inside her.

When it is time, the calf is born. Most calves are born in spring. A calf can stand and walk within an hour of being born!

Most mothers have only one calf each year, but sometimes they can have twins. Triplets are very rare but it does happen about one in every hundred thousand births!

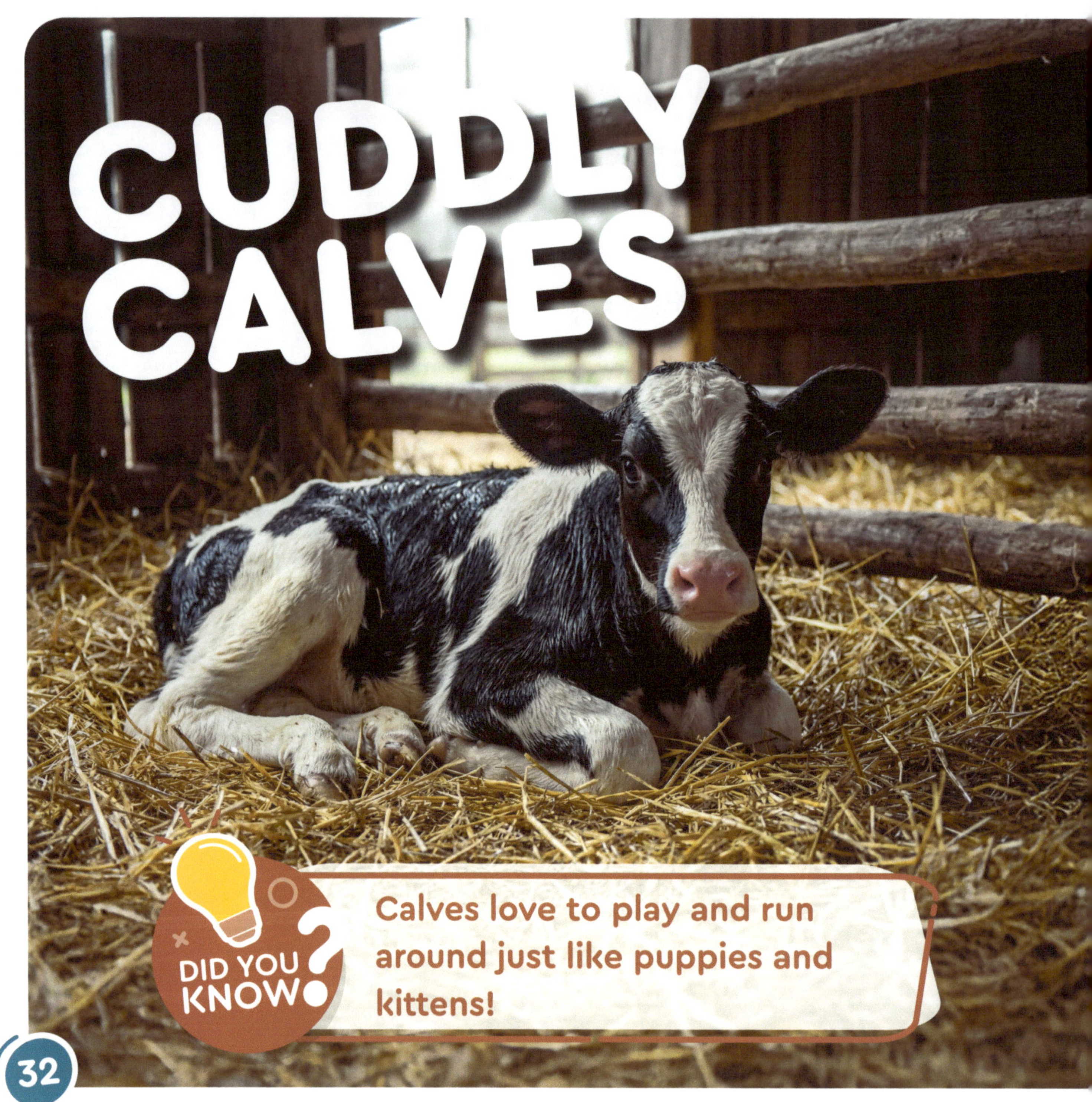

CUDDLY CALVES

DID YOU KNOW?

Calves love to play and run around just like puppies and kittens!

Plop! A wet, wobbly calf lies gently on the warm soft straw.

Newborn calves are small but tough. The mother licks them clean right away. Soon the calf finds her milk and starts to drink.

Baby calves drink milk from their mothers. They nurse many times a day. After a few weeks, calves start nibbling on grass too.

Calves grow fast. They can gain about two pounds every day. In just one year, a tiny calf becomes a big, strong young cow. They can weigh over 800 pounds by their first birthday!

CARING COWS

Huff! A mother cow breathes on her newborn calf to keep it warm.

Mother cows are fierce guards of their calves. They stay close and watch for danger. If danger comes near, a mom cow will charge!

Angus cows are known for being great moms. They nuzzle and cuddle their babies often. This keeps the calf feeling safe and loved.

As the calf grows, the mother teaches it what to eat. She shows it where to find water. Step by step, the calf learns to take care of itself.

Some mother cows will adopt and care for a calf that is not their own!

HARD
WORKERS

Creak! A strong ox pulls a heavy cart down the dirt road.

Cows have helped people for thousands of years. Long ago, they pulled plows across fields. Farmers worked the land by hand before using cows.

Today, cows still help in many ways. They give us food, milk, and leather. In some places, cows still pull carts and carry heavy loads.

Cow **manure** is helpful too. Farmers spread it on their fields. It makes the soil rich so crops grow tall and strong.

DID YOU KNOW? In some countries, dried cow manure is used as fuel to make fires!

BEST BUDS

Plod, plod! A Jersey cow walks slowly over to greet a new goat.

Cows share the farm with many other animals. They live near chickens, horses, goats, and sheep. Most cows get along well with their farmyard neighbors.

Some cows and horses become real pals. They graze side by side in the same field.

People and cows form bonds too. A farmer who is kind and gentle can earn a cow's trust. Some cows even enjoy a good scratch behind the ears!

Cows that have a best friend are calmer and can give more milk!

GLOSSARY

herd
A group of cows that live and move together.

cud
Food that a cow brings back up to chew again.

stampede
When a large group of animals suddenly runs in fear.

manure
Animal waste, or poop, that can be used to help plants grow.

graze
To eat grass slowly in a field.